To my little daughters
Nicole and Anna-Maria.
May they travel the world
and make it a better place

MISHI AND MASHI GO TO GREECE by MARY GEORGE
Published by MNG Publishing

www.mishiandmashi.com

No part of this publication may be reproduced in whole or in part, or stored in a retrieval system, or transmitted in any form or by any means, electronic, mechanical, photocopying, recording, or otherwise, without written permission of the author. For information regarding permission, write to mary@mishiandmashi.com .

Text & illustration copyright © 2020 by Mary George
Illustrations by Lisa Sacchi

All rights reserved

MISHI AND MASHI GO TO GREECE

Mishi and Mashi Visit Europe Series

Mishi and Mashi's family are going on a trip to sunny Greece. They have packed the car with bath-suits, inflatable toys, a canoe, fishing rods, cameras and everything else they need for a fun summer holiday.

"Mummy, where is this big boat taking us?" Mashi is curious.
"This boat is called a ferry, and it's taking us to an island. A piece of land surrounded by sea. Greece has thousands of them!" Mummy explains to the girls.

"Mum, Dad, look at the dolphins, they're dancing!" The girls point at the water.
"They're welcoming us to Greece," Mummy says, enjoying the show.

The family arrive and are welcomed to a beautiful villa by their host. "Kalimera, I hope you like olives," the kind lady says cheerfully, pointing to the trees which surround the villa. "These are olive trees."
"Can we pick some right now?" the girls ask. The landlady laughs and explains that olives can't be picked and eaten directly. They need to be prepared first.

Once unpacked, they hurry to the beach – of course! The girls play on the rocks all day, while Daddy paddles with the canoe and Mummy drinks frappés– a typical cold coffee. It is such a fun day for everyone, but they're getting hungry.

They head to the taverna -
a local restaurant with delicious food.
They eat seabass, octopus, shrimps
and even seashells!

Over the week, the family explore Greece. Their first stop is Santorini — a beautiful island with white and blue houses and churches.

"I've seen so many pictures with this view, Mishi, let's use our selfie sticks!"
The girls take pictures and have lots of fun.

On the island of Zakynthos, the girls see a shipwreck and a whole family of tortoises, resting in the sun. They want to pick them up and play, but a local boy appears.

He explains that the tortoises can't be **picked up** because it's not allowed. "My name is Apostolous," he says with a friendly smile. "I can show you how we have fun in Greece."

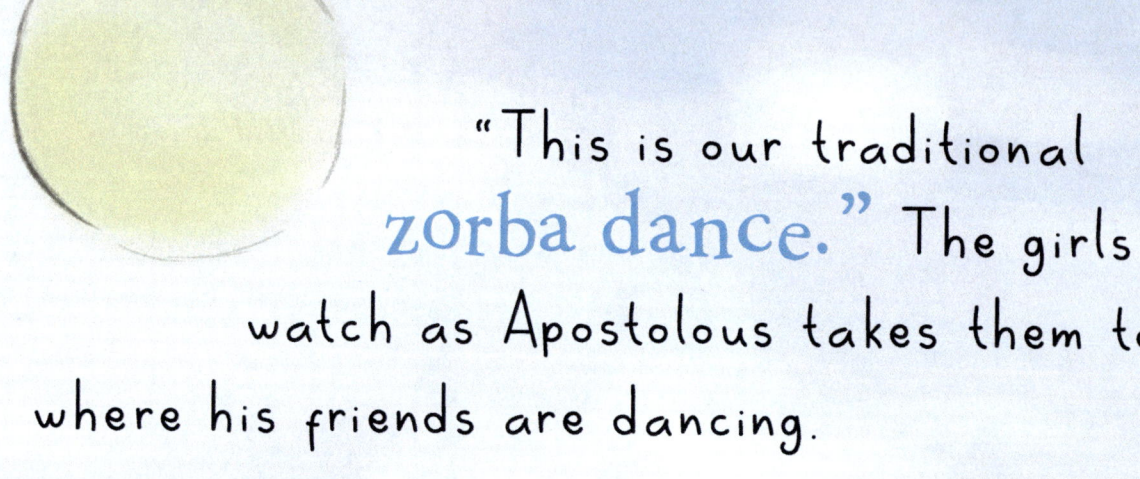

"This is our traditional zorba dance." The girls watch as Apostolous takes them to where his friends are dancing. "This is my favourite instrument, the bozouki, I'll play it for you."

The music Apostolous plays is very lively.
"This looks so much fun! Let's try it, Mishi!"
The girls join in the dance.

"We're going to Athens next!" Mashi grins.
"I hope we see Athena!" says Mishi.

"Girls, here we are at the splendid
Acropolis in Athens,"
Daddy says as they arrive.
"Is this the home of Athena?" Mashi is interested.
"Yes it was, a long, long time ago," Daddy replies.
"I understand why she moved out,
it's so old." Mishi nods.
They all laugh. The girls are ecstatic
to find Athena's statue.

On their last day, they visit the old Olympic stadium in Athens.
"Daddy, what are these Olympic games? I thought adults are boring and don't play games." Mashi is puzzled.
"Hehe, not so boring. The games include tennis, football, running, jumping... and many more sports. Every country in the world competes in them," Daddy explains.
"Greece was the first ever country to host the Olympics!"

It has been a fun holiday, but is time to go home. Mishi sighs and stamps her foot.
"It's so sunny in Greece, I want to stay here forever!" she cries.
Mum tries to cheer her up. The host lady says goodbye and gives them a pot of delicious olives for the journey.
"Antio, See you again soon!"

Great job! The Tortoise!

Now, let's learn some facts about it:

- **Greek tortoises** live on the ground. Turtles live in water. Do you see the difference?
- The tortoises' shells are hard, but be careful, they can feel pain through them!
- The tortoises, living in Greece, **only** eat grass and herbs
- The biggest population of tortoises in Greece is on the island of **Zakynthos** (yes, the girls met a whole family of tortoises there!)
- Some tortoises live as long as **300 years!**
- These sweet animals are under **high protection** in Greece. It is forbidden to take them out of the country (although Mishi really wanted to!)

Collect the other books in the series
Mishi and Mashi Visit Europe

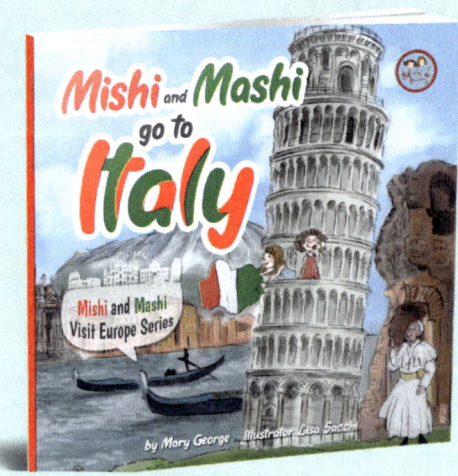

Made in the USA
Middletown, DE
19 July 2021

44465698R00020